WILDLIFE VIEWING AREAS

Rhode Island Ecoregions

Northeastern Coastal Zone

Landforms in the region include irregular plains, and plains with high hills. Appalachian oak forests and northeastern oak-pine forests are the natural vegetation types. Land use now mainly consists of forests, woodlands, and urban and suburban development, with only some minor areas of pasture and cropland.

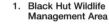

1. Black Hut Wildlife Management Area
2. Florence Sutherland Fort and Richard Knight Fort Nature Refuge
3. Powder Mill Ledges Wildlife Refuge
4. Watchamocket Cove
5. Touisset Marsh Wildlife Refuge
6. Audubon Society of Rhode Island Environmental Education Center
7. Emilie Ruecker Wildlife Refuge
8. Sakonnet Point
9. Norman Bird Sanctuary
10. Dutch Island Wildlife Management Avenue
11. Pettaquamscutt Cove National Wildlife Refuge
12. Tri-Pond Park Nature Center
13. Trustom Pond Refuge
14. Frosty Drew Nature Center
15. Block Island National Wildlife Refuge
16. Lathrop Pond Wildlife Refuge
17. Long Pond Woods
18. Fisherville Brook Wildlife Refuge
19. Big River Management Area
20. George B. Parker Woodland
21. Wickaboxet Management Area
22. Nicholas Farm Management Area

Most illustrations show the adult male in breeding coloration. Colors and markings may be duller or absent during different seasons. The measurements denote the average maximum length of species from nose/bill to tail tip. Butterfly measurements refer to wingspan. Illustrations are not to scale.

Waterford Press produces reference guides that introduce novices to nature, science, travel and languages. Product information and hundreds of educational games are featured on the website: www.waterfordpress.com

To order, call 800-434-2555. For permissions, or to share commer... editor@waterfordpress.com. For info... custom-published products, call 800... or e-mail info@waterfordpress.com.

120108

ISBN 978-1-58355-697-9 $7.95 U.S.

UPC

RHODE ISLAND WILDLIFE – An Introduction to Familiar Species

A POCKET NATURALIST® GUIDE

RHODE ISLAND WILDLIFE

An Introduction to Familiar Species

SEASHORE LIFE

Moon Jellyfish
Aurelia aurita
To 16 in. (40 cm)
Commonly washed up on beaches after storms.

Green Sea Urchin
Strongylocentrotus droebachiensis
To 3 in. (8 cm)

Common Sea Star
Asterias forbesi
To 10 in. (13 cm)
May be tan, brown, orange or olive with orange highlights.

Atlantic Bay Scallop
Argopecten irradians
To 3 in. (8 cm)

Eastern Oyster
Crassostrea virginica
To 10 in. (25 cm)

Sand Dollar
Echinarachnius parma
To 3 in. (8 cm)
White, shell-like 'skeletons' often wash up on shore.

Blue Mussel
Mytilus trossulus
To 4 in. (10 cm)
Grows attached to pilings and other marine objects.

Soft-shelled Clam
Mya arenaria
To 6 in. (15 cm)

Knobbed Whelk
Busycon carica
To 9 in. (23 cm)
Note prominent knobs on spire.

Common Slipper Snail
Crepidula fornicata
To 2 in. (5 cm)

Northern Quahog
Mercenaria mercenaria
To 5 in. (13 cm)
Found in mud near low tide mark.
Rhode Island's state shell.

Green Crab
Carcinus maenas
To 3 in. (8 cm)

Blue Crab
Callinectes sapidus
To 9 in. (23 cm)

Northern Lobster
Homarus americanus
To 3 ft. (90 cm)

Horseshoe Crab
Limulus polyphemus
To 12 in. (30 cm) wide

BUTTERFLIES

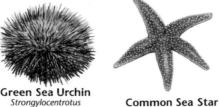

Eastern Tiger Swallowtail
Pterourus glaucus
To 6 in. (15 cm)

Orange Sulphur
Colias eurytheme
To 2.5 in. (6 cm)
Note prominent forewing spot.

American Copper
Lycaena phlaeas
To 1.25 in. (3.2 cm)
Common in disturbed areas and along roadsides.

Mourning Cloak
Nymphalis antiopa
To 3.5 in. (9 cm)
Emerges during the first spring thaw.

Eastern Tailed Blue
Everes comyntas
To 1 in. (3 cm)
Note orange spots above thread-like hindwing tails.

Red Admiral
Vanessa atalanta
To 2.5 in. (6 cm)

White Admiral
Basilarchia arthemis
To 3 in. (8 cm)
Common in upland deciduous forests.

Monarch
Danaus plexippus
To 4 in. (10 cm)

Great Spangled Fritillary
Speyeria cybele
To 3 in. (8 cm)
Common in marshes and wet meadows.

Spring Azure
Celastrina ladon
To 1.3 in. (3.6 cm)
One of the earliest spring butterflies.

Cabbage White
Artogeia rapae
To 2 in. (5 cm)
One of the most common butterflies.

Common Wood-Nymph
Cercyonis pegala nephele
To 3 in. (8 cm)

Pearl Crescent
Phyciodes tharos
To 1.5 in. (4 cm)

Silver-spotted Skipper
Epargyreus clarus
To 2.5 in. (6 cm)
Has a large, irregular silver patch on the underside of its hindwings.

American Lady
Vanessa virginiensis
To 2.5 in. (6 cm)
Underside of hindwings feature prominent 'eyespots'.

Underwings

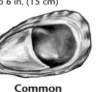

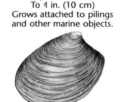

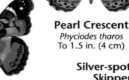

FISHES

Rainbow Trout
Oncorhynchus mykiss To 44 in. (1.1 m)
Note reddish side stripe.

Brook Trout
Salvelinus fontinalis To 28 in. (70 cm)
Reddish side spots have blue halos.

Scup
Stenotomus chrysops
To 18 in. (45 cm)

Northern Pike
Esox lucius To 53 in. (1.4 m)

Weakfish
Cynoscion regalis To 3 ft. (90 cm)
Back is covered with small spots.

Bluefish
Pomatomus saltatrix To 43 in. (1.1 m)
Short first dorsal fin has 7-8 spines.

Largemouth Bass
Micropterus salmoides To 40 in. (1 m)
Note prominent side spots.

Bluegill
Lepomis macrochirus
To 16 in. (40 cm)

Common Carp
Cyprinus carpio To 30 in. (75 cm)
Introduced species.

Striped Bass
Morone saxatilis To 6 ft. (1.8 m)
Has 6-9 dark side stripes.
Rhode Island's state fish.

Brown Bullhead
Ameiurus nebulosus To 20 in. (50 cm)

Yellow Perch
Perca flavescens To 16 in. (40 cm)

Summer Flounder
Paralichthys dentatus
To 3 ft. (90 cm)

Crappie
Pomoxis spp.
To 16 in. (40 cm)

REPTILES & AMPHIBIANS

American Toad
Bufo americanus
To 4.5 in. (11 cm)
Call is a high musical trill lasting up to 30 seconds.

Bullfrog
Rana catesbeiana
To 8 in. (20 cm)
Call is a deep-pitched – *jug-o-rum*.

Wood Frog
Rana sylvatica
To 3 in. (8 cm)
Note dark mask.
Staccato call is duck-like.

Gray Treefrog
Hyla versicolor
To 2.5 in. (6 cm)
Call is a strong, resonating trill.

Spring Peeper
Hyla crucifer
To 1.5 in. (4 cm)
Note dark X on back.
Musical call is a series of short peeps.

Green Frog
Rana clamitans
To 4 in. (10 cm)
Single-note call is a banjo-like twang.

Red-spotted Newt
Notophthalmus viridescens
To 6 in. (15 cm)

Yellow-Spotted Salamander
Ambystoma maculatum
To 10 in. (25 cm)

Eastern Painted Turtle
Chrysemys picta To 10 in. (25 cm)
Note red marks on outer edge of shell.

Snapping Turtle
Chelydra serpentina To 18 in. (45 cm)
Note knobby shell and long tail.

Eastern Ribbon Snake
Thamnophis sauritus
To 40 in. (1 m)
Slender snake has 3 distinct stripes.

Common Garter Snake
Thamnophis sirtalis To 4 ft. (1.2 m)
Brownish snake has yellowish back stripe.

Northern Water Snake
Nerodia sipedon To 4.5 ft. (1.4 m)
Note dark blotches on back.

Northern Black Racer
Coluber constrictor
To 6 ft. (1.8 m)

Milk Snake
Lampropeltis triangulum
To 7 ft. (2.1 m)

Smooth Green Snake
Opheodrys vernalis To 26 in. (65 cm)

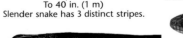

Canada Goose *Branta canadensis* To 45 in. (1.14 m)

Mute Swan *Cygnus olor* To 5 ft. (1.5 m) Introduced resident species.

Mallard *Anas platyrhynchos* To 28 in. (70 cm)

Northern Pintail *Anas acuta* To 30 in. (75 cm)

Wood Duck *Aix sponsa* To 20 in. (50 cm)

American Coot *Fulica americana* To 16 in. (40 cm)

Great Egret *Ardea alba* To 38 in. (95 cm) Note yellow bill and black feet.

Killdeer *Charadrius vociferus* To 12 in. (30 cm) Note two breast bands.

Great Blue Heron *Ardea herodias* To 4.5 ft. (1.4 m)

Snowy Egret *Egretta thula* To 26 in. (65 cm) Note black bill and yellow feet.

Sanderling *Calidris alba* To 8 in. (20 cm) Runs in and out with waves along shorelines.

Green Heron *Butorides virescens* To 22 in. (55 cm)

Common Tern *Sterna hirundo* To 15 in. (38 cm) Note black cap and forked tail. Orange bill is black-tipped.

Great Black-backed Gull *Larus marinus* To 32 in. (80 cm) Told by large size and dark back.

Laughing Gull *Leucophaeus atricilla* To 18 in. (45 cm)

Northern Bobwhite *Colinus virginianus* To 12 in. (30 cm)

Ring-billed Gull *Larus delawarensis* To 20 in. (50 cm) Bill has dark ring.

Wild Turkey *Meleagris gallopavo* To 4 ft. (1.2 m)

Ring-necked Pheasant *Phasianus colchicus* To 3 ft. (90 cm)

Ruby-throated Hummingbird *Archilochus colubris* To 3.5 in. (9 cm)

Rock Pigeon *Columba livia* To 13 in. (33 cm)

Downy Woodpecker *Picoides pubescens* To 6 in. (15 cm) The similar hairy woodpecker is larger and has a longer bill.

Northern Flicker *Colaptes auratus* To 13 in. (33 cm) Wing and tail linings are yellow.

Common Nighthawk *Chordeiles minor* To 10 in. (25 cm) Often hawks for insects around street lights.

Great Horned Owl *Bubo virginianus* To 25 in. (63 cm) Call is a resonant – hoo-oo-oo, hoo-oo.

Mourning Dove *Zenaida macroura* To 13 in. (33 cm) Call is a mournful – ooah-woo-woo-woo.

Red-tailed Hawk *Buteo jamaicensis* To 25 in. (63 cm)

Osprey *Pandion haliaetus* To 2 ft. (60 cm)

Turkey Vulture *Cathartes aura* To 32 in. (80 cm) Note two-toned underwings.

White-breasted Nuthatch *Sitta carolinensis* To 6 in. (15 cm)

Eastern Phoebe *Sayornis phoebe* To 7 in. (18 cm)

Tufted Titmouse *Baeolophus bicolor* To 6 in. (15 cm)

Barn Swallow *Hirundo rustica* To 8 in. (20 cm) Note deeply forked tail.

Black-capped Chickadee *Poecile atricapillus* To 6 in. (15 cm) Name-saying call is – chick-a-dee-dee-dee.

Carolina Wren *Thryothorus ludovicianus* To 6 in. (15 cm) Note white eyebrow stripe and wing bars.

Tree Swallow *Tachycineta bicolor* To 6 in. (15 cm)

American Robin *Turdus migratorius* To 11 in. (28 cm)

Eastern Bluebird *Sialia sialis* To 7 in. (18 cm)

Blue Jay *Cyanocitta cristata* To 14 in. (35 cm)

American Crow *Corvus brachyrhynchos* To 22 in. (55 cm) Call is a distinct – caw.

Common Grackle *Quiscalus quiscula* To 14 in. (35 cm)

Northern Mockingbird *Mimus polyglottos* To 11 in. (28 cm)

Gray Catbird *Dumetella carolinensis* To 9 in. (23 cm)

Cedar Waxwing *Bombycilla cedrorum* To 7 in. (18 cm) Red wing marks look like waxy droplets.

European Starling *Sturnus vulgaris* To 8 in. (20 cm)

Evening Grosbeak *Coccothraustes vespertinus* To 8 in. (20 cm)

Baltimore Oriole *Icterus galbula* To 8 in. (20 cm)

Red-winged Blackbird *Agelaius phoeniceus* To 9 in. (23 cm)

Scarlet Tanager *Piranga olivacea* To 7 in. (18 cm)

Northern Cardinal *Cardinalis cardinalis* To 9 in. (23 cm)

Eastern Towhee *Pipilo erythrophthalmus* To 9 in. (23 cm) Cheerful song is – drink-your-tea or drink-tea.

Dark-eyed Junco *Junco hyemalis* To 7 in. (18 cm)

American Goldfinch *Spinus tristis* To 5 in. (13 cm)

House Finch *Carpodacus mexicanus* To 6 in. (15 cm)

House Sparrow *Passer domesticus* To 6 in. (15 cm)

Virginia Opossum *Didelphis virginiana* To 40 in. (1 m)

Eastern Red Bat *Lasiurus borealis* To 5 in. (13 cm)

Eastern Cottontail *Sylvilagus floridanus* To 18 in. (45 cm)

Southern Flying Squirrel *Glaucomys volans* To 10 in. (25 cm)

Red Squirrel *Tamiasciurus hudsonicus* To 14 in. (35 cm)

Eastern Chipmunk *Tamias striatus* To 12 in. (30 cm) Note white stripes on side and face.

Woodchuck *Marmota monax* To 32 in. (80 cm)

Eastern Gray Squirrel *Sciurus carolinensis* To 20 in. (50 cm)

Norway Rat *Rattus norvegicus* To 18 in. (45 cm) Brown to gray rodent has a naked tail.

House Mouse *Mus musculus* To 8 in. (20 cm)

Common Muskrat *Ondatra zibethicus* To 2 ft. (60 cm) Aquatic rodent has a naked tail that is flattened on its sides.

American Beaver *Castor canadensis* To 4 ft. (1.2 m)

Striped Skunk *Mephitis mephitis* To 32 in. (80 cm)

Common Porcupine *Erethizon dorsatum* To 3 ft. (90 cm)

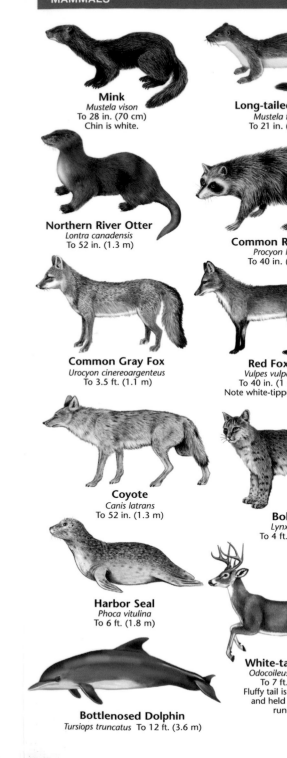

Mink *Mustela vison* To 28 in. (70 cm) Chin is white.

Long-tailed Weasel *Mustela frenata* To 21 in. (53 cm)

Northern River Otter *Lontra canadensis* To 52 in. (1.3 m)

Common Raccoon *Procyon lotor* To 40 in. (1 m)

Common Gray Fox *Urocyon cinereoargenteus* To 3.5 ft. (1.1 m)

Red Fox *Vulpes vulpes* To 40 in. (1 m) Note white-tipped tail.

Coyote *Canis latrans* To 52 in. (1.3 m)

Bobcat *Lynx rufus* To 4 ft. (1.2 m)

Harbor Seal *Phoca vitulina* To 6 ft. (1.8 m)

White-tailed Deer *Odocoileus virginianus* To 7 ft. (2.1 m) Fluffy tail is white below and held aloft when running.

Bottlenosed Dolphin *Tursiops truncatus* To 12 ft. (3.6 m)